Facing Up

Judith Mattison

FORTRESS PRESS   PHILADELPHIA

Library of Congress Cataloging in Publication Data
Mattison, Judith N.
  Facing up.
  I. Title.
PS3563.A86F3   811′.5′4   79-7385
ISBN 0-8006-1368-6

7704E79   Printed in the United States of America   1-1368

To Doug and Marcie Wallace
beloved friends
who foster much of my thinking
and accept me as I am

CONTENTS

PREFACE

This book is about feelings, because we all have them.

This book is about honesty, facing up to our real selves.

This book is about Jesus, who understands the human struggle.

This book is about life, and how every moment truly has meaning, even if we don't understand it.

This book is about you and me —
   people trying to be honest with ourselves,
   wanting to know God in every experience of life,
   wanting to love life,
   wanting to participate, like Jesus, in all life experiences.

This book is an attempt to help us look at all our experiences — good, sad, confusing, mysterious —

And recognize that we can grow to better understand and appreciate God's gift of life if we are willing to face inward and upward.

Potential

When I was born,
If I'd known my potential capabilities,
I would have been amazed!
I've been taught to be modest
And I sometimes notice my mistakes
*   more than my credits.*
So I have overlooked, ignored,
*   played down my attributes.*
Besides, if I admit my strengths
Someone will surely ask me to help,
*   and I haven't time.*

Five talents, two, or only one.
You expect me to use, to multiply—
*   even only one.*
Not because I should but
*   because I can! I'm able!*
You'll back me up if I falter a bit.
But you and I can multiply talents.
Amazing!

I'm Only Human

I am confused.
Sometimes I feel very strong
   powerful
   independent.
I make good decisions.
I lead other people.
I sing!

Other times I feel small
   a tiny creature
   walking on a huge planet
   small steps
     mistakes
     weariness
     fear.
I create and try,
But then I hesitate, hold back.
I assure a friend, but also
   weep at my disappointment.
I give up on life, but also
   smile.
In all this I sometimes categorize
My feelings and choices
   "good," "bad."

The fact though is I'm human.
I'm not consistent but
*   I search*
*   to grow through any experience,*
To discover
Some little truth about life
*   which will refill me*
*   and help me go on.*

I do not search alone;
You are there
*   you know*
*   you have felt, too.*
You understand.

Appearances

I'm affected by appearances.
   "Clothes make the man."
   "Every woman wants to look her best."
I want to be clean and pleasant-looking—
   I wouldn't want to throw away
   God-given health or gifts.
But when I fool myself about appearances
   I'm in trouble.
What I call "personal pride" in me,
   in another I call vanity.
I wear expensive clothes
   for an ego boost:
Yet, when I capitulate to those
   whose suits are fine
   and whose hearts are hard-finish,
I lose sight of humanity.

You strip me, Lord, of affectations,
   uninspired goals of temporary self-esteem.
You show me that my coverings
   do not change my essence.
My dignity is in your caring for me,
   whatever robe I wear.

Fear

I handle fear
By avoiding funerals
    and telling my children to be brave.
I seldom run across a storm severe enough to
    leave my knees weak
    or my eyes in tears.
I've come to rely on technology —
    a car can get me through a snowstorm —
And anyway,
Tragedy is for other people.
I'm afraid to be afraid.

You showed the disciples
    what it is to cope with fear.
In storms and death
You did not pretend false confidence
But encouraged them and me
To face the fear honestly
And lean
    in need
On you.

Worry

It's very unrealistic
To suggest that I not worry.
Look at all the fuel available
To burn in worry fires —
   kids and drugs
   peace and war
   traffic jams and rising interest rates.
It's a wonder I've any strength left.

On the other hand,
When has worry successfully
   replaced action?
Or produced energy for solutions?
When has worry untangled traffic?
Or given me a good night's sleep?
Worry is my stubborn need
To try to solve or understand —
   control all things.
Foolish me!
That's your job, not mine.

Projection

The things in me
I hate the most
I often see
In someone else.
   "She's petty."
   "He's impatient."
   "They're greedy."
   Not like me.
Even Adam tried it:
   "Eve told me to do it."
As with Adam
You offer me the chance
To be honest with myself
   and you,
To stop projecting, blaming
To confess the truth that
   I am but human,
   and you are God.
I have only to admit the truth
And you will welcome me,
   forgiving.

Anger

Sometimes I'm not sure
What I should do about anger.
On the Mount, Jesus told us
    not to be angry with anyone.
So I tried being "not angry."
It doesn't work.
I get mad! I get angry!
    Sometimes I even rage!
When I keep anger hidden, pretend,
    act understanding, rationalize,
    wait till it fades before I speak,
The anger doesn't go away at all—
    it changes into
    resentment, seething, sarcasm,
    or quiet ulcers, eating at me.
Then I live a lie.

Jesus was once so angry
    he overturned tables, yelling!
Paul said, "Be angry but do not sin . . . "
So that's it!
Anger is natural, real.
    It's me.

What I do with it is what counts.
If I hide it, deny it,
  I choose dishonesty.
If I spread it around to others,
  yell, quarrel, seethe,
  I'm not reconciled,
  I'm maintaining and enjoying anger.
But if I choose to admit my anger,
  say aloud, "I'm angry,"
  ask for forgiveness, speak my needs,
I have the opportunity to grow
  to be forgiven
  to straighten misunderstanding,
To acknowledge I am human
  and in need of Something Greater—
In need of God.

Sorrow

I knew I couldn't escape sorrow —
   my day would come —
But I deluded myself,
   thinking it might not hurt.
I am in pain
   an aching, stretching longing —
   empty, yet sharp and long.
I can only cry desperately
   then sadly
   and pray you stay beside me.
This pain, after all,
   is me.
It's part of my life
   because I have cared
   and I have been loved.

You know this feeling, Lord,
   for you have loved.
You understand that love is worth even pain.
I will go on —
   embrace these feelings,
Knowing that my awareness of my sadness
   brings me closer to you.

Hate

Strong word, hate.
It doesn't belong to me —
    not to me.
I dislike or feel annoyed.
I am moved to feel
    disagreement
    disappointment
    irritation.
Hate's too strong for me.

I know I'm hiding from the truth.
If I have strength enough to love
I also know the power of hate.
Call it by another name,
    yet it is me, my weakness.
You knew, you know,
And ask me not to run away
    or deny.
You ask only that I confess
    and begin again.
You forgive me.

Guilt

I used to see pictures of people
Lying on beds of nails.
    Odd ritual, I thought.
But I am like them.
Stretched on my spears of guilt,
    I feel the sting of every mistake.
Perhaps I feel more righteous
    ritualistically recalling
    my shortcomings.
But I come short of your Plan
    in not forgetting
    not letting go.

I would surrender to the truth
    of my fallibility;
    you are the Perfect, not I.
Self-punishment melts in the light of love,
    your acceptance.
My head rests on your bed
    of understanding forgiveness.
I sleep, peaceful.

Defensiveness

Someone offered helpful advice.
I bristled
   and scurried through my mind
   to explain my choice,
   my error.
I was defensive.

I protect myself from admitting wrong.
Sometimes because I need to feel right,
More often because
   I cannot bear to be wrong
   again.
Admitting another wrong
   would add to the lengthy list
   of my imperfections,
   which I tally daily.
I am defensive because
   I do not
   forgive
   myself.

Aging

Aging is for other people,
   except now and then
   when I can't run the stairs.
Gray hairs bother me.
But I feel just like I did when I was twenty!
   I feel young.
I have to feel young.
There isn't an ad on television
   that doesn't suggest
   I "should" be young.

If I admit I'm aging
   then I must acknowledge
   I'm dying.
I'll die someday.
   But not yet, Lord!
   Not so soon!
I'd rather pretend I'll be young forever.
Help me be more honest.
Life is the good gift
   and aging is
   the process of living.

Pressure

I live with pressure.
Responsibility, high expectations.
Sometimes I lie awake
   aware of my stiff neck,
   aching head, lower back pain.
Other times, I hardly notice
   when my stomach tightens,
   my arms stiffen,
   my hand clenches a pencil
   or grasps too hard in handshake.
I live with pressure.

I can't seem to let go.
   I need to achieve,
   be busy, check details.
And besides, I like work.
Or is it deeper than that?
Perhaps I prefer pressure to
   trusting
   failing
   sitting still and thinking
     about myself,
     my life.

Perhaps pressure is a way of
*   escaping my feelings about life.*
If I'm busy enough,
*   I won't feel deeply.*
*   I can avoid the possibilities of*
*   pain, disappointment, doubt.*
On the other hand, I will also miss
*   spontaneity*
*   a rush of love or laughter*
*   and a chance to learn from error.*

Pressure.
Help me look carefully at it, Lord.
At how much is inevitable
*   how much I choose to create,*
*   and how long my body*
*   and my spirit can endure*
Pressure.

Play

It's a blessing to be able to play.
There is nothing so freeing
As the flushed-out feeling I have
   after a set of tennis
   or a crazy table game
   or a long laugh with friends.
A ski slope quickens me.
Cold, rushing air and a sense of
   being close to you outdoors.

Play. Play!
Not watching but
   giving and trying
   laughing
   doing.
This is what life is meant to be —
Involving myself in it.
I am refreshed,
   my body more relaxed and healthy,
   ready for the serious part of life,
After a day or even an hour
Of play!

I'm Right

I am smug at feeling right.
My smile is falsely kind,
    understanding.
It's satisfying to have the answers,
    to be in charge.
I might even enjoy
    rubbing it in for pleasure.
Superiority.

I can't find a single time, Lord,
    when you were smug.
You knew infinitely more than we,
You understood the mystery,
    yet took no delight in being right.
Instead, you sought ways to show,
    told stories about God.
Your actions, completely right,
Supersede my misguided need
    for self-righteousness and superiority,
And prove me wrong.

Success

I like success.
Who doesn't?
It feels good
    and inspires me and others.
Have I begun to worship success?
It's a gradual, subtle logic
Where I believe that
    a good Christian gets rewards
    and a good worker goes to church.
Utilitarian faith—
    "Love God and he loves you."
    "Turn defeats into victories"
        (like Jesus did).
    "Rise to new heights in the Lord."
Success theology.

And you, Jesus,
    ignored all that.
Resurrection was deeper than victory.
It was sharing, struggling,
    knowing misunderstanding with people,
    and reunion with God.
Not so much success
    as giving.

Do I dare worship
  the struggling
  searching
  giving person,
The one who risked and felt
  failure?
Yes, I can worship one
  who was willing to abandon success
  in hope of reunion, reconciliation,
  and love.

Obedience

I know little of obedience.
Bowing and acquiescing
   belongs to servants,
   children.
I'm an adult.
   I make my own judgments.
When I must submit to
   the chain of command,
   I complain
   or chip away, go around.
My chin tips upward.
I don't even obey
   my self-imposed diet.

You show me obedience and loyalty
   to disappointing friends
   to tradition, to right,
Obedience unto death.
I sigh to think how far I must go
   to be like you.

Yet perhaps I would learn
    I would grow
    I would know more of life
If I were to obey,
Take a deep breath,
Tuck in my chin,
And begin —
    one step at a time.

How Difficult to Forgive

How difficult to forgive!
  to overlook, forget,
  pass by an opportunity to
    regain our "due"—
  to charitably construct the motives of
    a hasty reprimand
    a slight
    a cruel hurt.
How difficult!
Pride
  and self-righteousness
  would have me slash my way
  to justice—
    repaying or remembering
    keeping alive my bitterness
    regurgitating anger
    enjoying retribution.

Jesus blessed his enemies
  and bade me do the same—
    repay wrong
    with good.

Not that I am he,
    nor am I set above another
    in condescending charity.
I know my weaknesses.

Rather, I recognize that I am also one
    who selfishly destroys
    and feels ashamed.
I remember feeling relieved
    to have forgiveness;
I've sighed when mercy touched
    my bowing head.
And my self-respect would have me search
    for better than vindictive ways.
My loving God
    who has known all my errors
    and shown me mercy,
        human and divine,
Teaches me compassion.
"I forgive."

Disappointment

People let me down.
I have a new idea,
  they halfheartedly agree.
I plan a surprise,
  they don't show up
  or don't say thank you.
I wish them good luck,
  they forget my birthday
  or miss my hint for help,
  for praise.
People are a disappointment at times.

I need to look at myself
  and at life.
Do I expect too much?
Do I program people—
  thinking they will be happy
  just because I am,
  or wishing they will notice
  when I don't make an effort to inform?

Do I act strong
   and then feel hurt when no one comes
   to support my moments of weakness?
People are human,
   not perfect
   not mind readers.
They are no less self-centered than I.

I will look to Jesus for my example.
Like him, I would try again,
   believe in others
   offer second chances
   make my needs known
And continue to
   give to
   believe in
   care for
   and hope for
The best in people.
You did it, Lord.
I'll try too.

Helping

I like to do nice things for people—
  give a little gift
  or a special compliment
  lend a hand.
It makes me feel good to help.
I learned it from Mother and Dad.
They must have praised me whenever I
  helped.
I like to help
  because people will like me,
  and I need their approval.
I also enjoy being on top—
  not superior, really,
  just "good."

Keep me honest, Lord.
I can do much in your name
  for your people
Because I can love.
I can serve others, but not for me.
For them.
For you.

Generosity

I enjoy being generous.
It's easy with
    outgrown clothes
    or money to spare.
It makes me feel important
    or nice —
People like me.

You show me
Generosity means more than
    remnants
    or surplus.
Generosity means
    giving away
    what I'd prefer to keep.
That's hard.
Perhaps I have more to learn.
Teach me, Lord.

Games

I have a new device
    for getting along with people.
Whenever I lack courage
    to raise a question
    or make a suggestion
    or speak my anger,
I make a little joke
    an innuendo
    a cheery
        but double-edged comment.
I wait to see how others react—
Test the waters,
    feel them out,
    then laugh away their doubt.
    "I was only kidding."
It confuses others
    but it saves me
    from being honest,
    from risking failure
    disagreement
    rejection.

You knew nothing of such games.
You spoke truth
  even to those in authority
  and to pompous religious leaders.
You were honest
  with yourself
  and with others,
Knowing truth
  would overcome all games.

Winning

I need to win.
From Little League to checkmate
I prefer to be on top.
Sometimes I will even flirt
   with dishonesty
   in words or rules
To know the feeling of victory again.
The only loss I can bear
   is one I have decided to give away —
   patronizing, paternal.

I need the confidence that
   feeling disappointed
   achieving little
   feeling "less"
Will not destroy or weaken me;
Are opportunities
   to overcome and endure.

You know more of these things than I, Lord.
You had victory in hand
   and knew it.

You did not patronize me,
condescendingly restrain your strength.
You showed me true strength:
You chose to share
all feelings, all experiences —
victory, defeat, and understanding.
Your decision is my source of
inner strength.
I need not win to survive —
Only share in you.

Strong

Strong.
I have been strong.
Not a superperson
   but able.
The tennis ball
   bounced to my right
And suddenly
   in a zigzag flash of pain
I am weak.
Stopped.
I cannot run
   or twist,
   or even walk for a while.
Inconvenience bows
   to the greater trial
   of impatience
And my frustrated anger
To discover I'm not in control
   or strong.
Only human, Lord.

Endings

Life is full of unfinished things—
*   dangling participles*
*   separation*
*   vague memories*
*   and a yearning to tell*
*   those we cannot find*
*   that we're sorry.*
The puzzle is never complete
Because we're part of
*   the human condition.*
We are not able
*   to finish everything neatly.*
But we are able
*   to be part of the picture,*
Knowing you have seen it through.

Peer Pressure

When we talk about teenagers
We lament the weight of peer pressure.
Youngsters sometimes coax
    or goad or tease.
They watch each other carefully.
Some follow, unthinking,
    the examples of their peers.
Kids need to feel they belong.
It's hard to stand alone
    for what one believes.
It's easier to join the crowd.

It's not a teenage problem.
Peer pressure's not just for kids.
We are easily led by
    and hesitant to disagree with
    neighbors, friends,
    pastors, co-workers.
It's hard to stand alone.

We check around before deciding
  how to vote
  what to wear
  who to hire
  and when to laugh.
We want approval too.

Jesus was a sterling contrast
  to our capitulation
  to the popular.
He didn't sell out
  even in small matters
  (which have a way of growing large).
Jesus knew
  who he was in a crowd,
  and when to lead
  and when to follow.
Jesus was without peers.

Relaxation

It scares me
That I've forgotten how to relax.
So often I can unwind
    only if I'm far away
    and sometimes, even then,
    I'm sitting with body stiff and tense.
I'm accustomed to being
    responsible
    serious
    hardworking.

I've been taught
   in church,
   at home,
   and by our productivity-oriented culture
That to be worthwhile
   I must produce.
When I sit around
   I feel guilty.

I'm tired of it, Lord.
I'm tired of the fact that
   there will always be more to do.
I'm tired of driving myself so hard.
Help me understand that
   relaxing
   laughing freely
   "letting go"
   resting
Are not only good for my body
But essential for my soul.
I can love life more
   if I can trust it,
   if I allow myself the joy of
Just being me,
   human and acceptable.

Questions

The longer I live
The more I realize
The questions never end.
Once, not long ago,
    I asked someone
    about a Bible passage —
    something I'd never thought of
    quite that way before.
Her brow wrinkled;
    it was a new idea.
Perhaps it was heresy,
her look seemed to say.
    Don't ask.
Was it heresy to wonder?
Is it wrong to question?

In times when I'm torn with confusion,
    pain, dissatisfaction,
    or worse,
    with a sense of meaninglessness in life,
I question life itself,
    then wonder,
Is it wrong to question?

Or is it true
That wanting to know is
the beginning of learning,
and perhaps of wisdom?

I can live in tension
not being sure of meaning
wanting to find the glory
hoping to have revealed to me
the Purpose behind the event.
The tension refines my coarse understanding.
The desire to know may bring new joy.
The wondering and questions
may not be heresy at all—
They may be God, speaking
in a still, small voice
to me.
I wonder.

A Rational Person

I am a rational person.
My intelligence is at least average
and my logic even more acute.
I can find proofs for many things
and I have found my methods for
establishing reasons to believe.
Jesus, for example.
He's historical.
And the zeal of his followers
gives cause to wonder.
He certainly was a superior being,
even equal to God.
God. I figured that out too.
God is nature
and love and the great Causer.
Things had to start someplace, I figure.

But then I met tragedy
mystery
uncanny coincidence
and a rising sense inside me
that there is something greater
than what I can see, touch, and reason.

I can't explain it,
    but it is there.
It's real.
In fact,
    it's the only thing that lasts.
Everything else I know disappears—
    buildings, people, forests,
    scientific explanations.
Only the unseen qualities of life remain.

I realize that if I could prove or reason out
    that there is God,
What I proved
    would not be God at all.
It would be me,
    thinking as big as I could.
Just me.
Only Jesus makes God understandable.

Tragedies

There are things we can't explain.
The death of a mother,
  five young children
  left behind and insecure,
  and three years later
  the father dies.
A child
  autistic
  uncommunicative,
  and the daily drain
  on her mother.
Accustomed to our scientific method,
We concoct our formulas —
  cause, effect
  stimulus, response.
All it does is tidy up our mind.
The spirit wants:
Why?

You understood the mystery
  of intellect too small
  and lives too short
  to understand.
You told us
  believe without seeing.
Help us learn to
  release the need to know,
To live
  one day at a time
  trusting
  satisfied to be alive
  and in your Plan.

Happiness

I've been looking for happiness
   for years—
Some combination of
   things and people
   knowledge
   security and success.
But it doesn't work.
Problems still come up,
   boredom, losses, questions.
I get cynical:
   "Happiness is a bad joke."
I begin to see that
   happiness isn't measurable,
   predictable, attainable.
Life doesn't reach some sort of peak.
Few events make us deliriously happy.

There are better goals.
   Paul talked of being content in all.
   David, of knowing ourselves.
   Jesus said satisfied, blessed.
It must have something to do with believing
   that all events have meaning,
   all people are part of a Plan,

the qualities of Life—
trust, love, truth, goodness—
are present among us.
Happiness surrounds
an honest search for Being,
for meaning in our lives,
and trusting
that Goodness and Truth survives
because it is of God.
Not delirious, but genuine.
Not a reward, but a Way.

Dying

Even in my strongest times
I'm not too keen on dying.
Even you cried out—
 you felt abandoned,
 and the others cried.
You knew this was the
Ultimate human battle
 reconciling life and death.
So you let yourself
 experience it all.

It really is too great
 for me to understand.
Dying
 is a mystery.
I can't deny or escape it.
Thank God,
 you lead the way.

Hope

The elusive spirit of hope
will not be confined.
It is larger than wishes,
for wishes lack courage
and change before our eyes.
Hope waits.
It doesn't prescribe answers,
only believes
that answers exist
even without our knowledge.
Hope risks change
or wrong choices.
It survives without proofs,
despite terror.
Hope embraces even misery,
Believing there is purpose
and that spring will come.

Security

We thought we'd feel secure
  when we bought a home.
We're homeowners now.
But it doesn't work.
  You can't buy security.
I thought I'd feel secure
  when I got married.
It's nice and comfortable
  but not secure.
People die or change.
Houses burn and oaks wither.
We haven't got the strength we had
  when we were young.
Nothing brings security.

Maybe that's one of the hardest lessons
  life teaches us:
Nothing is secure.
We can't tie things down, predict.
  "Here today, gone tomorrow."

We keep trying
in tangible, purchasable ways
To get a corner on security.
But like mercury it slips away —
self-assurance quivers
patterns change
people move.
We haven't faith that's deep enough —
the security of believing
God is present in all things.
We try to compensate with human concepts,
and it doesn't work.

You knew it was a problem for us.
Over and over you repeat
God cares
God stays
God loves
Believe.

Morality

I kept thinking
It would all come out
  in black
  or white —
That there are simple final answers.
Someone would tell me what's right.
Now I see
  morality
  is trying to distinguish Truth
  from all the murky gray.
Making a decision
  whether ultimately
  right
    or wrong
Is the honing of morality.
No one else
Can do it for me.

Worship

I sit in my place, waiting to be fed.
A seal, with my mouth open
  stiff-necked, slick and smooth.
I wait for someone else to give.
I want a message for the week.

David experienced worship.
He wept despair, pouring out himself—
  questioning, challenging,
  actively waiting.
And he sang joy!

I would participate like David.
I would hear,
  sing,
  say aloud,
  feel the words of leaders, friends, myself.
I would enter into the moment,
  feel your presence,
  take home more than pulpit messages.
I would know God!
I would worship.

Separation

I never like separation.
Even in unpleasant situations,
  leaving
    always feels like loss.
Peter knew.
His whole body and spirit
  must have wept
  to see you dying,
    leaving him behind.
It's not easy, separating.
We need other people.
We miss their presence,
  if not their affirmation.

What does it teach me, Lord?
That change
   may not be comfortable
   but need not destroy.
New friends emerge
   or familiar relationships are enriched,
   more dear, as we comfort each other.
We learn
   that death or leaving
   can be less a loss,
   more a gain,
If we recognize that each new path,
   like winter,
   can lead to new growth
   rebirth
   resurrection.

Trust

The Bible's full of promises.
I have only to trust God,
   not me and my arrangements.
Trust God.
I have a long way to go.
I deny your power by
   traveling and living in
      familiar places
   befriending only folks
      like me
   passing up opportunities
      to change.
That way I don't have to trust
   anyone but myself.

It's hard to trust people.
   Especially those I don't know.
When people earn my trust,
   I give it.
But that's rewarding good behavior,
   that's not trust.
There is no virtue
   in trusting the trustworthy.

You're looking for more, Lord—
Trusting even doubtful characters,
Trusting in unfamiliar places—
    cities, neighborhoods, churches.
Trusting life and your Plan
    even when I feel uncomfortable,
    even before it works out.
Trusting the unseen.
Trusting God.

Future

Predictions —
  weather
  stocks
  politics
  and our next vacation.
A slip on rainy pavement
  and all is changed.
I know I should live now,
  "Tomorrow never comes,"
  but I like to feel prepared.
With the possible exception
  of my own death
  I like to look ahead,
  avoid danger and problems
  plan the future.

Lord, if you had spent your energy
  predicting, planning
  scheming as I do
Would you have called the Twelve?
Ignored political power
  in favor of patient teaching

and the healing
of ordinary people?
You saw Future differently.
Future was not
    clocks, maps, annuities,
    and security.
Future was building on lasting truths
    right and justice
    love and loyalty
    patience with people
    caring for children
Every day.

Talent

We are in awe of certain talents.
Generally we praise
  artists, musicians,
  athletes, writers,
  gourmet cooks.
We suspect their work is effortless
  and call the abilities "gifts."

Perhaps we are too superficial.
Real talents may be
  the patience of mothers
  the kindness of business partners
  the love of a caring wife
    for her paralyzed husband
  the wisdom of those who've known pain.
The measure of talents
  is their use or development —
  how we share them.
They are gifts
  not because they are devoid of hard work,
But because they are shared!

Patriotism

I'm loyal to my country.
Imperfect as it is at times,
I believe in its goodness
   its possibilities
   its hope.
We are blessed people.
But you have not blessed us
   because we are good
   or special.
Rather, we are humbled
To realize the goodness
   you give us
   is free,
   without merit.
If we are strong
   or kind or true
It is because you allow it.
We seek to return it all
   in example.
Our loyalty is to you.

Clearance Sale

Passing by the item in the store
Was difficult
Because it was on sale — clearance.
It grew large before me
    all its uses
    the beautiful colors
    the unique design
And my desire to have,
    possess, acquire,
    purchase
Grew to an emotion-charged pitch.
I approached the salesclerk
    only to discover
I could have two for even more savings.
    Two!
I began to plot how I could use two
    where I could store them
    who I could tell
And to compliment myself
    on thrift and wisdom,
    being in the right place
    at the right time.

Suddenly, I knew.
Wrong place, wrong time.
I didn't really need one
certainly not two.
I was trapped
in bondage (in a "free" country)
To the desire to have more and more,
to satisfy emotions
rather than needs.
I redefined.
"Wisdom" was really my "wanting"
and my "thrift"
was simple greed.

I walked away.
Wrong place.
Wrong time.
Wrong reasons.
Wrong god.

Unvarnished

I stripped a piece of furniture
   to its natural wood.
Removed layers of shiny varnish,
   dirt and dust of years of use.
The wood beneath was fine,
   solid, true.
I stripped my life of its unnecessary varnishes.
I kept my family and closest friends,
   a simple home, basic food,
Knowledge that I'm able to
   contribute to the world,
     part of God's Plan, a Reason to live.
Stripped of all the other things—
   lobster with melted butter
   matching end tables
   a boat and a new car
   a ring to remember our anniversary
The substance remained,
   solid, true,
   fine, unvarnished—good.

Wealth

Rich
   is other people
With enough to spare,
   to spread around.
I will not claim wealth.
It requires responsibility —
   sharing, giving
   gratitude
   satisfaction.
I prefer striving
   increasing, gaining
   reaching for more
Claiming I'm still
   so far behind the others.

Today I shall pile upon my camel
   all my possessions,
   gifts and talents
And count them one by one.
Will my camel fit
   into the needle's tiny eye?

The Pleasure Seekers

There have been books and movies
About pleasure seekers.
They're portrayed as
  drug addicts
  sexually active people
  "wild."
But I'm a pleasure seeker too.
Not that I'm immoral—
  not blatantly.
I just arrange my life
  to accommodate my desires.
I like thrills and excitement
  and I often pay well
  to be entertained.
I eat sumptuously.

The ad-people have discovered
I buy products that promise
  satisfaction of my desire for pleasure:
  I buy cars driven by
    beautiful women and virile men.
I like words like
  convenience, ease, glamour,
  luxury, and important.

And chemicals—
I'm told
life would be impossible without them.

My greatest pleasures lately were
watching children giggling
helping a neighbor
reading a fine book
soup and sandwiches
sitting quietly by the fire.
Not marketable pleasures,
not always convenient or easy,
But real.

Inefficiency

I get angry at inefficiency.
I've been taught
   and have developed habits
   of careful, thoughtful action.
I think it's irresponsible
   to do otherwise.
I am peeved
   when helping agencies
   or the government
   are less than efficient,
   using slow, expensive methods.
Business wouldn't stand for that.

Help me to be more discerning,
To recognize the difference between
   slow and patient
   irresponsible and caring.
People aren't like ledgers,
   easily balanced
   everything neatly arranged.
Helping and changing takes time.

Jesus knew that.
I can't think of a situation
    when he was in a hurry
    to make his next appointment.
He listened
    and waited and encouraged.
People need that
    because we're human
    complicated
    resisting change
    and in need of comforting care.

Thanks for lessons
    which challenge my hasty,
    businesslike values
And remind me of Jesus—
    patient
        even slow
    but magnificently efficient
Because he truly loved us.

Space and Life

We are descendants of pioneer travelers
Who saw open land and limitless space
As something to be overcome,
  subdued, and filled.
Blessed with much
They took it, used it.

We, like they, expect to find
More.
More space, more trees, more water,
  more things.
We claim our territory,
  our section of land,
And demand our privacy,
Our personal space —
Although it is no longer limitless,
  but a luxury.
We expect wilderness to survive
  without planning.
We consume voraciously,
  ignoring the needs of posterity.
We buy bigger,
  add on, expand.

Then we fill our extra space
With things
And wonder that we use so much energy
Replacing things and making
More.

Jesus understood that life
Is simple,
That it is relationships —
    love and anger
    cooperation and listening and time.
Space and separateness are not superior to
Knowing each other better.
Space is a luxury of temporary withdrawal.
Life
    is love
Close together.

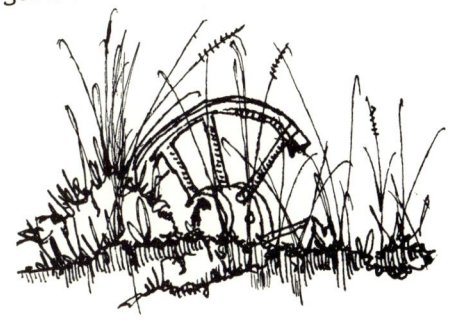

Food

My meal was delayed two hours.
My body and mind reacted—
   weary, headachy, irritated.
I'm accustomed to regular meals,
   and snacks and desserts.
I suppose for the majority—
   the other two-thirds of the world—
Promptness isn't the issue.
They get beyond headaches,
   stomach pains, irritation.
Theirs is lethargy and loss of hope,
   unending misery
   for their unsuspecting children.

Not only is it not fair
   it is not right
And I know there is something
   you want me to do.
You would have it done—
   you did it.
Lead, Lord.

Special

There has been an emphasis lately
    on helping people realize they are
    worthwhile,
    loved and lovable just as they are.
But in the process
    we've sometimes come to feel that
    we are special.
We're "looking out for number one."
We have battered the Golden Rule,
    commitment, compassion, patience,
    loyalty, and acceptance
In the name of doing our own thing.

There is a balance somehow
    where I feel fulfilled, respected, accepted,
    and I offer the same to others.
The balance is in Jesus
    who loved all, sought reconciliation
    was committed through hardship and pain,
    neither denying
    nor flaunting his strengths—
Looking out for Number One
    and for me.

Small Differences

Theologically
  they're not like me.
Or at least their terms are different
And their mannerisms, background.
I'm uncomfortable with them.

Perhaps that's how the people felt
At the first Pentecost:
Surrounded by differences—
  languages, gestures.
There was so much excitement,
  confusion, and noise
That I probably would have
  avoided the crowd.
  (I prefer private meditation,
  orderly services, English.)
Still, someone in that group
  would have spoken my language,
Because everyone needed to hear.

When messages sound different,
  the Spirit may be the same.
Perhaps I need to listen
  more care-fully.

Listening

I know active listeners
  not by their ears
  but by their eyes.
They are the ones who
  don't avoid my gaze
  who stand still, lean in,
  nod, and wrinkle their brows.
They are the ones who care.

You listened
  without imposing
  your personal prescriptions
  of what others ought to be saying, doing.
You spoke
  only when they had finished speaking
  and in words and stories
  they could understand.
I, Lord,
  would be like you,
Accepting.

Sex

One thing
We seldom discuss in church
Is sex.
Not only did Victoria
*   make it a dirty word,*
We pretend it doesn't even exist!
We don't cast stones at lust—
*   we pretend it isn't there*
*   on television commercials and the*
*   February cover of Sports Illustrated.*

As we search with friends for meanings
*   in Scripture or in life,*
*   couples seldom admit or share*
*   that it can be hard*
To physically say, "I love you"—
That our bedrooms can be battlegrounds,
*   or frozen-meat lockers,*
*   no-man's-lands, or actors' stages.*
Afraid to talk, we foolishly accept
*   the words of experts or reports*
And don't discover
*   what is natural, real—*
*   perhaps even "normal," like the others.*

Single or married, we give sex
   a heightened meaning.
Misuse of sex is "super sin"
And liking it is suspect.
Problems with it are taboo.

The same old problem, Lord.
We keep thinking we must be perfect
And we tend to doubt you'll understand.
I shake my head at myself.
I've forgotten how often you tried to teach
   through the forgiven adulterer, David
   the loving Magdalene
   the love songs of Solomon
   and the woman at the well.
You painted many pictures
   and showed us better choices.
You didn't ask us to match statistics
   or to pull the covers over our heads—
Only to be loving
And to ask you how to do that best.

Prisons

It's easier to scold
   criticize, second-guess
Than it is to help constructively.
Prisons of the state,
   full of tears.
Prisons of poverty,
   people who begin every day
   one, two, twenty steps behind—
   never catching up.
Prisons of sickness
   or loneliness
   or the discomfort of the
   socially inept.
I'd rather criticize than change.
I'd rather subtly gloat
   as if superior
   than reach out and help.
Then I wonder,
What if you are in the prison?

Insulation

I bought insulation the other day —
Not for my house, for me.
I avoided a part of town
    poor, old
Because it reminds me that
    I am fortunate
    and others are not.

Sometimes my insulation
    is isolation, airspace.
I need time alone
    in my car, my room,
    with my thoughts.
Jesus needed isolation too
    prayer, quiet, away from crowds.
But he used that privacy
    to equip himself
    for reaching out.

Rather than avoid and be insulated,
I would reach out and be warm.

Untouchables

We've virtually conquered leprosy.
Lepers are gone
 or treated and healed.
But we have lepers all around us,
 untouchables.
Some of them are old
 and no one touches them any more
 because they aren't very attractive
 and we feel distressed
  when they cry
  or complain
  or can't handle simple functioning.
They make us feel helpless
 and afraid to die.

No, Lord,
 we choose to feel helpless
 and afraid to die.
We could choose, as you did, to feel
 compassionate
 helpful
 caring.

We could bring a touch of kindness—
   an understanding voice—
   to those who feel tired
   discouraged
   ashamed of inadequacy
   alone
   or unaware of reality.
We could hug them
   as we hug children
   who have the same need for acceptance.
We could bring healing and life
   because we can give love
   out of the well of goodness
   you have given us.
We can choose to touch,
   and in your name
   comfort and assure,
   help heal the spirit.

Marriage Solutions

When we were children
We played by rules
  hide-and-seek
  softball
  Out! Safe!
We'd argue loudly over close calls.

Now I'm married
And close calls
  gray areas
  individual needs
Upset the flow.
Solutions and decisions
  are no longer determined
  by referees and rules.
I often try to solve our conflicts
  with win-lose terminology.
Win and lose is familiar
  but out-of-date.
In marriage, to win or to lose
  is not the issue or the goal.
The issue and the goal
  are reconciling,
  and understanding.

Early Arrivals

I move through life rapidly,
   timing stoplights
   filling calendar squares.
It's our way of life.
Up early, rush to work
   activities, steady pace
   rush home, quick meal, evening out
   hurry to bed in order to get up early.
No time left
   to read, to sit, to think
   to watch the children grow.

It's our way of life
   fueled by petrol, possessions,
   and meaningless stimulation
And destined to destroy humanness.
We hurry by the impact of being alive
   and arrive early
At our spiritual
   and physical
   graves.

Together

We are created to be
Together.
From the start
We have been linked to others—
  conceived by two
  loved by many
  and invisibly part of a
Far-reaching world of humanness.
We are bound together,
  sharing the tears of the hungry
  the dances of children
  the frustrations of the oppressed
  and the fallibility of each, of all.
We cannot make all things good,
Yet together we can share,
  learn, care, work to change,
And contribute to a growing Good,
Blessed by God.
We can be part of God's Plan,
Together.